50 Quick Ways to Ir

Ma

By Mike Gershon

About the Author

Mike Gershon is an expert educationalist who works throughout the UK and abroad helping teachers to develop their practice. His knowledge of teaching and learning is rooted in the practicalities of the classroom and his online teaching tools have been viewed and downloaded more than 3.5 million times, making them some of the most popular of all time.

He is the author of over 80 books and guides covering different areas of teaching and learning. Some of Mike's bestsellers include books on assessment for learning, questioning, differentiation and outstanding teaching, as well as Growth Mindsets. You can train online with Mike, from anywhere in the world, at www.tes.com/institute/cpd-courses-teachers.

You can also find out more at www.mikegershon.com and www.gershongrowthmindsets.com, including about Mike's inspirational in-school training and student workshops.

Training and Consultancy

Mike offers a range of training and consultancy services covering all areas of teaching and learning, raising achievement and classroom practice. He runs inspiring and engaging INSET in primary schools, secondary schools and colleges. Examples of recent training events include:

- Growth Mindsets: Theory and Practice – William Bellamy Primary School, Dagenham
- Creating a Challenge Culture: Stretch and Challenge Reimagined – Manchester College
- Rethinking Differentiation – The British School of Brussels

To find out more, visit www.mikegershon.com or www.gershongrowthmindsets.com or get in touch via mike@mikegershon.com

Other Works from the Same Author

Available to buy now on Amazon:

How to Develop Growth Mindsets in the Classroom: The Complete Guide

How to use Differentiation in the Classroom: The Complete Guide

How to use Assessment for Learning in the Classroom: The Complete Guide

How to use Bloom's Taxonomy in the Classroom: The Complete Guide

How to use Questioning in the Classroom: The Complete Guide

How to use Discussion in the Classroom: The Complete Guide

How to Manage Behaviour in the Classroom: The Complete Guide

How to Teach EAL Students in the Classroom: The Complete Guide

How to be an Outstanding Trainee Teacher: The Complete Guide

More Secondary Starters and Plenaries

Secondary Starters and Plenaries: History

Teach Now! History: Becoming a Great History Teacher

The Growth Mindset Pocketbook (with Professor Barry Hymer)

The Exams, Tests and Revision Pocketbook

Also available to buy now on Amazon, the entire 'Quick 50' Series:

50 Quick Ways to Get Past 'I Don't Know'

50 Quick Ways to Start Your Lessons with a Bang!

50 Quick Ways to Improve Literacy Across the Curriculum

50 Quick Ways to Improve Feedback and Marking

50 Quick Ways to Use Scaffolding and Modelling

50 Quick Ways to Stretch and Challenge More-Able Students

50 Quick Ways to Create Independent Learners

50 Quick Ways to go from Good to Outstanding

50 Quick Ways to Support Less-Able Learners

50 Quick and Brilliant Teaching Ideas

50 Quick and Brilliant Teaching Techniques

50 Quick and Easy Lesson Activities

50 Quick Ways to Help Your Students Secure A and B Grades at GCSE

50 Quick Ways to Help Your Students Think, Learn, and Use Their Brains Brilliantly

50 Quick Ways to Motivate and Engage Your Students

50 Quick Ways to Outstanding Teaching

50 Quick Ways to Perfect Behaviour Management

50 Quick and Brilliant Teaching Games

50 Quick and Easy Ways Leaders Can Prepare for Ofsted

50 Quick and Easy Ways to Outstanding Group Work

50 Quick and Easy Ways to Prepare for Ofsted

About the Series

The 'Quick 50' series was born out of a desire to provide teachers with practical, tried and tested ideas, activities, strategies and techniques which would help them to teach brilliant lessons, raise achievement and engage and inspire their students.

Every title in the series distils great teaching wisdom into fifty bite-sized chunks. These are easy to digest and easy to apply – perfect for the busy teacher who wants to develop their practice and support their students.

Acknowledgements

My thanks to all the staff and students I have worked with past and present, particularly those at Pimlico Academy and King Edward VI School, Bury St Edmunds. Thanks also to the teachers and teaching assistants who have attended my training sessions and who always offer great insights into what works in the classroom. Finally, thanks to Gordon at Kall Kwik for his design work.

Table of Contents

Introduction

Welcome to 50 Quick Ways to Improve Feedback and Marking. This book is all about the practical strategies you can use to improve the quality, impact and efficiency of the feedback you give and the marking you do.

These two aspects of teaching have a huge impact on students. Good, timely feedback which students understand and have a chance to implement can have a significant impact on achievement. Similarly, effective and efficient marking is essential if teachers want to gain a sound understanding of were their students are at, and want to modify and adapt their planning, teaching and future assessment accordingly.

We can think about feedback and marking as two sides of the same coin. While they are not identical, they are closely connected and share a lot of similarities. However, it is important to note that feedback can exist independently of marking – most often in the case of verbal feedback. Here, the role of marking is taken on by the teacher's real-time assessment of what is happening in the classroom. Marking, on the other hand, tends to be done subsequent to the event. It is a reflection on and analysis of the work students produced during the lesson.

There are many ways in which you can improve your feedback and marking. The fifty entries which follow will guide you through a whole host of these, on the way exemplifying and illustrating what implementation looks like. But don't think that what I have written is set in stone. You can take the ideas as they are presented and implement them. Or, you can adapt and modify them to fit your teaching style and your students. Either way, you will be well placed to develop your practice and help your students make great progress.

Why do feedback and marking matter?

01 Teaching can be loosely described as three separate processes – planning, teaching and assessment. The last of these includes feedback and marking. Assessment happens both during the lesson, when the teacher is assessing what is in front of them, and after the lesson, when the teacher is marking student work. Feedback can be provided in both situations. In-lesson feedback is likely to be verbal and post-lesson feedback tends to be written, though this is not always the case.

Feedback matters because it is an important way in which the teacher communicates with their learners. The content of this communication is crucial. It is the transference of expertise.

Teachers have expert knowledge and understanding. Their students do not – yet. The goal of teaching is to help students become more expert. Feedback allows us to do this. It is through feedback that we give students access to our expertise. They can then take this, use it and, over time, make it a part of themselves. Hence, feedback plays a significant role in directing and maximising the effectiveness of student learning.

The most important aspect of marking – why it matters most – is that it gives the teacher access to the student's current thinking, skills, knowledge and understanding. Two benefits accrue. First, armed with this knowledge the teacher is in a better position to tailor their teaching to meet student needs. Second, this information provides the basis for relevant, personalised feedback.

Not So Splendid Isolation

02 Feedback and marking should not take place in isolation. By this, I mean that they should not be seen as sufficient in and of themselves. If feedback is not implemented, its impact is severely diminished. If marking does not inform subsequent teacher behaviour (increasing the level of challenge, re-teaching a misunderstood idea, giving additional feedback and so on) then it also has less impact.

Splendid isolation is simply out of the question when it comes to marking and feedback. Both must be seen as part of the answer, not the full answer.

Feedback must be considered in conjunction with student actions around the information feedback provides.

Marking must be considered in conjunction with teacher actions around the information marking elicits.

I do not want to labour these points as we go through the book. Therefore, you should work under the assumption that when I talk about feedback and marking I am always doing so with these principles in mind. On occasion, I will make this explicit. Elsewhere, it will be assumed. In a few entries, such as number 41 – Target Implementation Time – our focus will fall entirely on the process of ensuring students act on the feedback you provide.

One final thought before we move on. To what extent are your learners aware that the feedback you provide is a tool for them to use? Something on which they can act in order to change their thinking, skills, knowledge or understanding?

It is worth reflecting on. The more aligned students are with this positive, productive view of feedback, the easier it is to get them acting on the feedback they receive.

Entry Slip Feedback

03 Here, then, is our first technique: entry slip feedback. There are at least two ways in which you can use this:

1. Prior to the lesson, write individual feedback for each of your students on separate slips of paper. This feedback should pertain to what students have done previously *and* what they will have the opportunity to do in the upcoming lesson. Do not feel you have to write something different for every student. It is likely that a number of students will benefit from similar – perhaps even identical – feedback. As students enter the room, hand them their entry slips. Ask them to read the feedback, discuss it with a partner, and be prepared to put it into practice during the lesson.

2. Prior to the lesson, create a set of ten targets for improvement which cover all the students in the class. For example, you might note down five targets which apply to twenty students, three which apply to the next eight and two which apply to the final two. Turn this list into an entry slip. Print off copies and hand them to students as they enter your room. Ask them to read through the lists, to discuss them with a partner and then to decide which target most applies to them. Indicate that this is the target you

expect them to pursue during the course of the lesson.

Two points to note before we move on. First, in the second example you may need to circulate through the room to check that students are selecting targets which are sufficiently challenging. Second, you will need to plan lessons which allow students to put their feedback or targets into practice, otherwise their efforts will be stymied.

Avoiding Trait-Based Praise

04 Here are some examples of trait-based praise:

- That's amazing!

- You're brilliant.

- What a genius.

- That is so smart.

- Wonderful – you always get it right first time.

Praise like this tends to be given with the best of intentions. The teacher wants to share their positive feelings with the student, in the belief that these will reinforce a positive sense of self.

However, research by Carol Dweck and others has shown that this is not always the result of using trait-based praise. In fact, praise of this type tends to create a brittle sense of self, causing a fixed mindset in which students assume there is something innate to them which causes them to create good work – as opposed to that good work being the result of processes such as effort, trial and error, attention to detail and so forth.

Instead of using trait-based praise, try to provide praise in which the approbation is tied to feedback indicating why the thing in question is good. This highlights to students that their choices and actions have led to good work being produced, not simply something inherent to them. Here are three examples of what this can look like:

- Great essay, John, I can really see how you spent time clarifying your thoughts before you started writing.

- I'm fascinated by this piece of work, Sylvia, can you talk me through why you decided to use mixed media instead of a single form?

- Lovely work, Ahmed, I can see from this that you tried a couple of different methods first before working out the best approach to take.

Feedback is a Gift

05 We give gifts without expectation of receiving something in return. We choose gifts based on what we think the other person would like, or what might benefit them. We know that there is a taboo around refusing gifts. If someone presents us with something, we nearly always accept. We know the social consequences of refusal.

Feedback is a lot like a gift. We give it to students without expecting anything in return (except, perhaps, that they make use of it). We give feedback which we believe will be useful to the student in question. Our feedback is based on what they can do and what we think they could do with a little assistance. When we give feedback, our aim is to provide a benefit to our learners.

Talking about feedback as a gift is one way to change student perceptions. It can help you to overcome the resistance to feedback some students show. Often those who see feedback as a threat, or some kind of negative commentary highlighting a perceived lack of ability.

This is a nice way to take the 'sting' out of feedback for these students. To neutralise some of the negative emotions they might associate with it. If using the technique, I would advise you to first talk to students about gifts and why feedback is a gift, using points similar to above, then to return to this metaphor on a regular basis, so that students become accustomed to thinking in this way.

Giving Access to Your Expertise

06 Another way to change how students think about feedback is to point out that it is simply the way in which you give them privileged access to your expertise. That expertise encompasses subject knowledge, wider cultural knowledge and knowledge about teaching and learning.

Many students will fail to think about feedback in this way unless prompted. They will not necessarily make the connection between you providing them with ways to improve and these ways being predicated on your expert knowledge and understanding. Explaining that feedback gives access to your expertise means explaining that the information students receive, in the form or targets and feedback, is especially powerful. It is expert information they can take and make a part of themselves. In so doing, they become more expert.

This is a very positive – and highly realistic – way to think about feedback. It does provide students with access to your expertise and it is designed to make them more expert.

A student who receives and implements feedback on a regular basis will draw closer to the teacher's level of expertise over the course of a year. While they are unlikely to match or surpass that expertise, they will get closer to it. And that, in short, is what learning is all about.

Pay Attention to Working Memory

07 Working memory is short-term memory. The memory we use to process information in the moment. Working memory is limited. It is widely held to be limited to seven pieces of information, plus or minus two.

A couple of important points follow.

First, we are usually at our most effective when we can focus all of our working memory on the task in hand. If we have to divide our working memory between a number of separate tasks, then we tend to suffer disproportionate declines in effectiveness. This is most true if the tasks are unfamiliar.

Second, there is only so much our working memory can do at any one moment. If it becomes overloaded then we are likely to withdraw from what we are doing, stop, and wonder what is going on. If we are self-aware, we will probably be able to identify that an overload has occurred. We are then in a position to do something about it – such as breaking a task down into manageable sections. If, however, we are not in a position to do this, as many students are not, then withdrawal may well signal the complete end of our engagement.

From this we can conclude that when you provide feedback to students you should pay attention to working memory. Do not give too much. Do not overload students with lots of different things. Personally, I would say one target at a time is enough. Students can then focus their full working memory on making sense of this and trying to implement it. When they've done so successfully, give them their next target, and so on.

One Thing At a Time

08 Here are some examples of how you can help students to focus on one thing at a time when it comes to feedback:

- Provide one target. As noted in the previous entry. This could be through verbal or written feedback. For example, you might circulate through the classroom during an activity and give some students a single target to focus on as they complete the activity. Another option is to give the entire class the same target on which to focus. This is particularly useful if similar mistakes are in evidence across the board.

- Give time in which target implementation is the primary focus. The premise is simple. If students are directing all their attention onto target implementation then they are likely to maximise the effectiveness of their efforts. In addition, you send a signal that target implementation matters; that it has high value in the classroom. Entries 41-44 develop this point further.

- Make students aware of what working memory is. Explain to them how working memory works, what its limitations are and, as a result, why it is beneficial to focus on one thing at a time.

- **Hold back.** You will often be tempted to give students lots and lots of feedback in one go. Hold back. Remember that you are an expert and know most, if not all, of what they aren't doing right or what they could do to improve. But also remember that they need to focus on one thing at a time. That if you give reams and reams of feedback it will be too much; and they will likely withdraw or disengage as a result of being overloaded.

Making Verbal Feedback Responsive

09 What is clear thus far is that feedback is a powerful tool through which to direct student effort. This brings significant benefits. Targeted effort is far more effective than random or poorly applied effort. Giving students the means through which to focus their efforts means giving them a way to make the most of the limited time they have with you in the classroom.

We can extend this principle to all instances of verbal feedback.

Making verbal feedback responsive is easily done. During the lesson, whenever an opportunity to deliver feedback arises, remind yourself that what you are about to say can, and hopefully will, target student effort. Doing this means reminding yourself that the content of your verbal feedback has an immediate impact – on student learning and on what the student chooses to do with the limited time they have available.

While this is unlikely to lead to vast changes in the feedback you deliver, it will hone your feedback to some degree, sharpening it up and ensuring that it is delivered with students' subsequent efforts in mind.

Working in this way means you are responding to what you see in front of you – what students are doing – but also to what you cannot yet see but want to see – what students will do next.

Show Me, Tell Me, Convince Me

10 How can you be certain that students have fully acted on your feedback? That they have both implemented your target and understood what you were asking them to do?

One approach to use is 'show me, tell me convince me.' It works as follows:

The teacher has provided students with feedback and has asked them to work on implementing this through the course of the lesson. During the first main activity the teacher circulates through the room and talks to a number of students. One student tells the teacher that they need a new target because they have already succeeded in putting their first one into practice.

Rather than giving a new target straight away, the teacher decides to test whether this is the case. They ask the student the following three questions:

- Can you show me where you've implemented your target?

- Can you tell me why that is an example of successfully putting your target into practice?

- Can you convince me that you have mastered the feedback and are ready to move on?

Notice how the difficulty of the questions gradually develops. In the second and third question, the onus is on the student to articulate their understanding – which doesn't always run in tandem with the act of putting a target into practice. Using this questioning technique you can quickly ascertain whether or not students have fully understood and assimilated your feedback.

Marking Codes

11 Marking codes are a way to speed up your marking. They also help students learn what to look for when assessing their own work. They work as follows:

Identify key areas on which you regularly give feedback, or in which students regularly make mistakes. Then, assign a code to each area. For example, an English teacher might identify the following:

- Grammar (G)

- Punctuation (P)

- Spelling (SP)

- Sense (S)

- Word Choice (W)

Having developed a code, you then need to tell students about it. Explain how it works, what you will use it for and why you are using it. Our English teacher, for example, might introduce students to the above code, before explaining that they will use it to identify things students should be able to correct themselves, meaning that the teacher can focus their detailed feedback on more substantial matters.

Over time, students will get used to a marking code. As part of this process, they will become accustomed to focussing on the items which constitute your code. They will thus develop a clearer sense of what they ought to be looking for when assessing their own work.

Colour Coding

12 An alternative to marking codes is colour coding. Here we use colours to quickly highlight areas of student work we feel they need to attend to. It can work in a number of ways, including:

- The teacher uses three different coloured highlighter pens to colour code areas of student work which are good, need improving and which would benefit from discussion between the teacher and the student.

- The teacher uses one colour to highlight a series of elements of a student's work, all of which demonstrate the same area for improvement. For example, a maths teacher might highlight five incorrect answers, all of which exhibit the same error.

- The teacher uses two colours. The first is used to highlight areas where the student could improve their work. The second is used to highlight one or two areas where they have avoided making the same error. Students are then able to contrast what they've done well with what they need to improve.

In each of these cases the student needs to do some follow-up work. The colour coding makes this easier by providing instantly recognisable visual information. Little interpretation is required. Instead, the student can go straight to what has been highlighted and start thinking about what they need to do next.

Whole-Class Target Lists

13 We've mentioned these in passing but they're worth thinking about in more detail. Here is an example of a whole-class target list from a sociology lesson:

1. Practice writing answers in which you first describe, then explain.

2. Use contemporary examples to support your argument.

3. Make connections between different agents of socialisation.

4. When explaining your answers, use a range of key terms.

5. Practice using keywords to explain your ideas.

6. Apply a combination of categories when analysing a question. For example, gender, ethnicity and age.

7. Use different theories to critique each other.

The list contains a set of targets which apply to the class as a whole. We might imagine that the teacher has shared this after marking a set of mock exams. Some of the targets are harder than others. Taken as a whole, the seven run the gamut from straightforward to challenging, reflecting the mix of abilities in the class.

The teacher has two options over how to use the list. First, they can display it on the board and invite students to look through their mocks and identify which target is most appropriate for them to pursue. Second, having marked the mocks, the teacher can run through them again and write a number between 1 and 7 on the front page of each, indicating which target the student should work towards.

Pre-Emptive Feedback

14 I would argue that in ninety percent of the activities we plan, we can predict in advance the type of feedback we will give to ninety percent of our students. This is even truer for experienced teachers than it is for teachers near the beginning of their careers.

It follows that we can plan pre-emptive feedback into our lessons. This is feedback which we know in advance will apply to the majority of our students. Here's an example:

A history teacher has set students a task which sees them analysing a set of primary sources connected to the Industrial Revolution. She knows in advance that students will probably fail to push their analysis to any significant depth on their first attempt and that many will not make connections between the primary sources and the work they've done in class over the past two lessons.

With this in mind she plans pre-emptive feedback to introduce halfway through the activity. This is a set of five targets, two covering the level of detail in students' analysis, two covering the making of links to existing areas of knowledge and understanding, and one focussing on evaluation (this being aimed at the most-able learners).

This approach allows the teacher to redouble students' efforts midway through the activity. Used regularly, it also serves to habituate students into a mode of thought which says that the first attempt is only that – the first attempt. There is always room for improvement.

Mistake Crib Sheets

15 Mistakes are fertile ground from which much feedback springs. Mistake-making is a standard part of learning; often it is a sign that the level of challenge is about right. After all, if you're not making any mistakes, the chances are you've mastered whatever it is you're working on.

Mistake crib sheets are a highly specific method for giving feedback, and they can be highly effective. Here's how they work:

Before you begin a unit of work, make a list of the common mistakes and misconceptions you see each time you teach this area. Or, if you haven't taught it before, look through your scheme of work and identify the mistakes and misconceptions you think students are likely to make.

Having done this, use your list to create a mistake crib sheet. This should contain the mistakes you have identified, alongside brief explanations of why they are mistakes and any key points they illustrate. Make copies of this and distribute to students, one each.

Next, talk students through the crib sheet. Use this as one of the first activities in the first lesson you teach on the topic. Explain that the crib sheet is feedback in advance of the event. You are showing students the mistakes they might well make, and giving them a means to spot these and then learn from them.

Students retain the crib sheet and use it through the course of the unit. You can also use it as the basis for discussions with individual students and as a tool to talk to the whole class about the learning.

Modelling Feedback Implementation

16 Some students don't know how to implement the feedback they receive. In other cases, a student won't understand the feedback you've given them. Both of these examples indicate that it is sometimes necessary for you to model feedback implementation. That is, you must show students both how to implement the feedback you've given them and what successful implementation looks like, in terms of the end product.

Here are some examples:

- A PE teacher demonstrates to a student how their head is falling back every time they shoot in basketball. They then demonstrate how to keep your head still while shooting, before asking the student to practice changing from the former to the latter.

- A primary school teacher demonstrates to a student how they are responding negatively when faced with difficult situations. They talk through the kind of feelings the student is experiencing and where these come from. Next, they demonstrate how to respond in a more positive manner, talking the student through the process of thinking about the situation and identifying a good choice to make.

- A science teacher demonstrates to a student how they are misreading a graph. They talk the student through the misconception and then show them a useful process to go through when reading graphs of this type, in order to ensure accuracy. The student is then invited to have a go under the teacher's supervision.

Feedback on Thinking

17 One of the most powerful types of feedback is feedback on thinking. This is because thinking underpins the actions in which students engage. So, for example, an essay is the result of the thinking a student has done both before and while writing their essay. Similarly, a piece of student artwork is a consequence not just of the physical movements in which they've engaged (such as moving a pencil across a piece of paper) but also of the thinking which has preceded or run concurrently with those movements.

Feedback on thinking helps students to look more carefully at the thinking in which they engage and to refine that thinking, changing it in line with the information you provide. This promotes metacognition which, along with feedback, has been shown time and again to be a highly effective tool for raising student achievement.

You can give feedback on thinking in many ways. Here are some examples:

- Ask students to try a different method or strategy.

- Ask students to drop a certain part of their thinking and replace it with something else.

- Ask students to change their thinking and to compare the results with what happened previously.

- Ask students to include some additional premise, idea or strategy as part of their thinking.

- Ask students to slow their thinking down so as to avoid careless mistakes.

Whole-Class Narration of Thinking

18 Staying on the theme of thinking, a useful technique through which you can give metacognitive feedback to the whole class sees you narrating your thinking in front of all your students. Here's an example:

A primary school teacher stands at the front of the room, next to the whiteboard. They display a maths problem on the board and show students how to solve this. As they do, they narrate their own thinking, articulating the thought processes they would use to make sense of, and ultimately solve, the problem.

The teacher then reveals a second, similar problem. This time they slow things down a little and spend longer talking through each step of their thinking. Finally, they reveal a third, similar problem. This one is accompanied by a step-by-step breakdown of the teacher's thinking.

Next, students are given a set of problems to try on their own. The teacher leaves the third slide on display, meaning students can turn to it for support while they are working.

In this example, we see the teacher giving feedback to the whole-class. The feedback comes in advance of them attempting the work. It is akin to the teacher saying: 'rather than having a go and seeing where your thinking takes you, let me give you feedback on how to think successfully about problems of this type, then you can try to apply that.'

Highlighting Differences

19 Consider these three teacher statements:

- 'You can see where you did it well there, but also where it went wrong, over here.'

- 'That's what a misapplication of the theory leads to. Have a look at this, which shows you what a correct application looks like.'

- 'Can you see the differences between these two pieces of work? What makes the first one better than the second?'

In each example, the teacher has found a way to highlight the differences between success and a lack thereof. In so doing, they give students really useful information; feedback they can take on board and use in the future.

Take the first example, the teacher is showing the student how their work demonstrates both success and failure. By highlighting the differences between these two elements they help the student to understand why one is better than the other, and what needs to be done to bring the latter in line with the former.

Highlighting differences can take a variety of forms. It can be done verbally or through writing. Whenever you choose to use it, ensure that students fully understand why the information is useful. Emphasise that a good understanding of difference, in the context of learning, is founded on a good understanding of what success entails.

Mental Contrasting

20 Mental contrasting is a strategy anyone can use to increase the likelihood they will achieve their goals. It involves recasting goals in the form of 'If...then...' sentences. The contrast is between the desired future and the things which must be done in the present to achieve this. Here are some examples of targets being turned into 'If...then...' sentences:

Target A: Practice using full stops to end your sentences.

If... then...: If I want to improve my writing, then I need to use full stops at the end of my sentences.

Target B: Watch the ball all the way onto the bat when you play a stroke.

If... then...: If I want to score more runs, then I need to watch the ball all the way onto my bat.

Target C: Taste your food as you cook and season it accordingly.

If... then...: If I want to cook tastier food, then I need to keep tasting and seasoning as I go.

In each example we see how the teacher's feedback is turned into a sentence over which the student has ownership. This ownership is closely tied to the connection made in each sentence between the desired goal and the process which needs to be pursued to achieve that goal.

All in all, mental contrasting is a helpful technique to teach students, allowing them to take control of the feedback they receive.

Categories – Part One

21 Categories are one of the key tools we use to make sense of the world. Along with concepts they form much of the bedrock of our thinking. How do I know this is a lesson? Because it accords, in large part, with the category of lesson as I have come to understand it. How do I know this is a good day? Because it seems to have the features of a good day and therefore fits into the 'good day' category.

We can use categories to help us mark more effectively. Here's how:

Sit down and make a list of between five and ten key categories you invoke when looking at student work. For example, an art teacher might note some or all of the following categories: Line, Shape, Colour, Precision, Proportion, Perspective, Scale, Originality, Tone and Structure.

You now have a set of lenses through which to look at student work. A set of categories through which to target your feedback.

Let us extend our example. The art teacher collects in work from all the students in his class. As he marks, he has his list of categories beside him as a prompt. Whenever he senses that he is uncertain over what feedback to give, he turns to his list, identifies an appropriate category and uses this to frame his comments. As a result, the process of marking becomes easier. The category list is like a cheat sheet, helping the teacher to give feedback more quickly than might otherwise be the case.

Categories – Part Two

22 You are an expert in the subject or subjects you teach. This is certainly true relative to your students and is probably true relative to most of the population as well. Being an expert, you have internalised knowledge and understanding which you use to make judgements about student work. A significant part of your judgement-making process is the invocation of categories.

Continuing our example from the previous entry, the art teacher may circulate through the room during an activity, look at student work and giving feedback. This feedback is informed by the categories which lie at the heart of the teacher's thought. So, for example, they might look at one student's work and give them expert feedback on their use of shape – invoking, as they do, their highly developed understanding of what constitutes good and not so good use of shape.

We can help students to become better judges of their own work by sharing with them the categories we use to make judgements. For example, our art teacher might ask his students to self-assess the piece of work they have produced, before handing it in for him to mark. As part of this, he would display on the board the set of ten categories we listed in the last entry. He would then ask students to select one or two of these to use as lenses through which to make their judgements.

Repeated use of this technique helps students to become more effective evaluators of their own work. It helps them to become more expert in how to look at work in a given subject.

Process Delineation

23 In Entry 21 we looked at how we can speed up marking by identifying in advance the categories we use to make judgements. Another helpful method sees us delineating into a series of separate steps the important processes we want students to use when producing their work. Here's an example to illustrate what this looks like in practice:

A Design and Technology teacher is marking a set of student projects. The students have been asked to create a light-meter. They have completed their projects and handed these in. The teacher, before starting to mark, sits down and delineates the design and build process they expect their students to have followed as part of the task. To start, they divide this process into five key elements:

- Planning

- Prototyping

- Revision of Plan

- Building

- Finishing

They then make a couple of notes next to each category, effectively subdividing them. By the end, they have five major processes, each subdivided into two minor processes.

This only takes a couple of minutes. But it gives the teacher a clear delineation of the overall process they have asked students to pursue. They can then use this as the basis of their feedback. Looking at each light-meter in turn, they ask themselves which part of the process has caused the student the most difficulty. Having identified this, they are quickly in a position to offer appropriate, accurate and tailored feedback.

On-Hand Criteria

24 A variation of the previous technique is to mark student work with a set of criteria on-hand. You can then refer to these as you go, meaning you don't have to keep the criteria at the forefront of your mind. Instead, you can rest assured that they are contained on the piece of paper next to you, or on the computer screen in front of you. This lets you focus all your attention on assessing the quality of student work and identifying the most useful feedback to give.

Here are some examples of the technique in action:

- A teacher sits down to mark a set of student books. They have success criteria from recent lessons to hand as they do this.

- A teacher is marking a set of essays. They have a mark-scheme nearby but have synthesised this into a set of five key criteria they can use to quickly assess quality.

- A teacher is observing students in a practical lesson. In advance of the lesson they printed off a short list of criteria to use as the basis of their judgements. They have these in their pocket, ready to use as necessary.

In each case, the teacher uses the criteria as a reference point to speed up the process of marking while ensuring they retain a high level of accuracy.

Mark with a Purpose

25 This seems obvious, but do you always do it? Sometimes we find ourselves marking student work in a manner which might best be described as aimless or, to put it more diplomatically, without clear purpose. We are marking the work because we have to, because it is expected. But how much better would the quality of that marking be – and how much more useful would it be to our students – if it was driven by a clear, guiding principle?

Here are some examples of what that might look like:

- A PE teacher marks student work with the express intention of identifying conceptual errors around the key ideas relevant to the topic.

- A primary school teacher marks student work with the purpose of identifying the extent to which all students are able to apply a given mathematical technique.

- A geography teacher marks student work with the purpose of giving feedback on the accuracy of their mapping skills.

- An economics teacher marks students work with the express intention of identifying misuse of statistics to support arguments being made in essays.

- A maths teacher marks student work with the purpose of identifying common misconceptions usually associated with this particular topic.

In each case, the teacher has made a decision in advance about what they are looking for. This primes their marking, helping them to focus their attention and leading to better results.

What do you want me to mark?

26 Try posing this question to your students and see what happens. You might be surprised by the results.

Asking 'what do you want me to mark?' means asking students to assess the quality of their own work. They need to identify what conveys the clearest sense of their current ability and skills. And they need to think about which pieces(s) of work are likely to draw the most useful or illuminating feedback from the teacher.

It is not always possible to use this technique. Everything depends on the type of work students have been producing and the volume of this work. They must have something to choose from – both in terms of relevance and range. Here are some examples of where the technique really comes into its own:

- In art a student has produced a whole series of sketches. The teacher asks them to select three of these to be marked.

- In English a student has written a raft of sonnets. The teacher asks them to look through their work and decide which two they want feedback on.

- In science a student has produced half a dozen model answers to 6-mark questions. The teacher asks them to identify which three they want feedback on.

- In geography a student has created a series of maps. The teacher asks them to select one on which they would like feedback.

- In dance a student has recorded themselves performing three different routines they've choreographed. The teacher asks them to decide which they think is best and then gives feedback on this one.

What do you want me to give feedback on?

27 A variation on the theme works as follows. Instead of asking students what piece(s) of work they want you to mark (see last entry), ask them which area of their work they would like feedback on. Indicate that they should make a note of this on whatever they have produced before handing it in to you.

This serves a few purposes. First, it lets you focus your feedback on something specific. Second, it encourages students to critically assess the quality of their own work. Third, it helps students to take ownership of their work. After all, they are deciding where feedback might be useful and then actively trying to elicit that feedback by communicating what they think to the teacher.

You can scaffold the activity through the use of categories (see Entry 22). For example, you might display a set of eight categories on the board, relevant to the topic you have been teaching, before asking students to choose the category about which they would most like feedback.

You can extend the activity by asking students to not only tell you the area on which they would most like feedback, but to also provide a justification of why they think this feedback might be useful or important. Here you are pushing students to articulate the rationale informing their decision-making.

What changes should I notice?

28 Our third and final variation on this theme. Try asking students 'what changes should I notice?' They should write the answer to the question on their work before they hand it in, or they should talk you through their answer before showing you their work.

In either case, the purpose is the same. We are asking students to examine what they have done and assess whether progress is truly evident, or whether they are in fact repeating the same mistakes they made previously.

This works particularly well when students have had an opportunity to implement a recent target. For example, a student might have written a story and, while writing it, attempted to put into practice their target of using a wider variety of adjectives. Asking 'what changes should I notice?' leads to them re-examining their work to identify where they have successfully implemented their target.

A couple of points follow. First, the teacher's job is made a little easier because the student is identifying changes in advance. Second, the student is actively engaged in assessing their own work and in comparing what they thought might be the case with what actually is the case. This can be revealing. Many students will find they have made fewer changes than they thought, or hoped. But knowing this is a good thing. They are then in a better position in the future to accurately judge the rate of change – or degree of target implementation – in which they truly engage.

Diagnosing Mistakes and Misconceptions

29 Mistakes and misconceptions offer fruitful ground from which to provide feedback. It is through mistakes and misconceptions that we are able to identify key areas in which student knowledge and understanding is shaky and/or incorrect. Diagnosing mistakes and misconceptions means finding ways to draw these into the open. You are then in a position to give feedback on them. Here are four examples of how to do this (a fifth, hinge questioning, is explained in the next entry):

- **Anticipate common mistakes.** You can predict in advance the kind of common mistakes you are likely to see over the course of a unit of work. Primed to think about these you are then more likely to spot them.

- **Use follow-up questioning.** This sees you pushing students to explain, clarify and add detail to their ideas. Through this type of questioning you can identify whether students are giving correct answers through sound or faulty reasoning. If the latter, you can give relevant feedback.

- **Plan tasks so they elicit mistakes and misconceptions.** Think about how the structure of a task gives students a chance to make mistakes or to reveal misconceptions under which they are labouring. How you plan the task can make it easier or more difficult to get these into the open.

- Ask students to identify mistakes and misconceptions. Give students copies of exemplar work, some of which should contain mistakes and misconceptions. Ask them to find these and to explain why they are not right. If they miss any, then this suggests they may be making the same mistakes or misconceptions themselves.

Hinge Questioning

30 In hinge questioning, the teacher poses a question based on the element of the learning on which all else hinges. If students have a secure understanding of this they can move on. If they don't, then the teacher needs to intervene, re-teach, discuss and give feedback which will help them to secure their understanding.

Here is an example of a hinge question:

Which of these items are magnetic?

A) An iron nail

B) A copper wire

C) A piece of glass

D) A plank of wood

The learning on which everything else hinges is the ability to correctly identify magnetic objects. If students have got this, fine. They can move on and build on it. If they haven't, we need to intervene. Otherwise they will be relying on faulty information as they go forward.

In the above example, (B) is deliberately included in an effort to catch students out. A common misconception when first learning about magnetism is that all metals are magnetic. The teacher has intentionally included this answer in an effort to bring misconceptions out into the open – a much better place for them to be than locked up inside students' minds.

Careless Versus Useful Mistakes

31 Distinguishing between careless and useful mistakes is a good way to give your marking a clearer purpose. It also helps students understand the difference between the two. Careless mistakes are those mistakes students make when they are not paying full attention or when they fail to adequately check their work. Useful mistakes are mistakes which give rise to a teaching opportunity, which elicit information which can be used to inform future efforts, or which reveal a misconception (from which the teacher can teach away).

Showing students the difference between these two types of mistakes means putting the onus on them to identify and correct their own careless mistakes. You can then focus on any useful mistakes you identify while marking – or, indeed, during the course of a lesson.

Feedback on useful mistakes is likely to be richer and more interesting than feedback on careless mistakes. It presupposes that the student is missing something from which they will benefit. Feedback on careless mistakes tends to involve the teacher reminding students of something they already know.

One option you might like to pursue is to create a handout or wall display illustrating the difference between careless and useful mistakes. Students can then use this as a reference point. Over time, they should come to internalise the exemplars, leading to a secure understanding of the difference.

Mid-Unit Assessment

32 Marking of student work often comes at the end of a unit. This is frequently done by means of an assessment. The teacher plans a piece of work intended to encompass all, or much, of what has been covered during the course of the unit. They then mark student work with the intention of identifying how much students have understood, how much they know and how successful they have been, overall, in terms of their learning.

There is nothing wrong with this. It is often a fruitful approach; one which helps both teacher and students. However, another approach is possible. One which leads to some quite different results.

This is mid-unit assessment. Instead of waiting until the end of the unit to assess where students are at, the teacher plans a piece of assessment work for half-way through (or, perhaps, for two-thirds of the way through). The aim is to elicit information about student skills, knowledge and understanding, and to give feedback on these, while there is still time to act.

For example, let us imagine a religious studies teacher is teaching a unit of work looking at the meaning, use and role of prayer in different religions.

They plan an assessment piece for half-way through the unit. The results of this are used to inform the rest of their teaching. Students also receive feedback which they can work on during the remaining lessons. The teacher concludes the unit of work by setting a second assessment piece.

Collating Mistakes

33 This technique is a handy way to give feedback about mistakes to all your students. It works as follows:

Over the course of a few weeks, a primary school teacher marks the numeracy work their students produce. As they do this, they set up an MS Word document in which to collate the common mistakes they are seeing. They then use this document as the basis for an activity.

Students work in pairs. Each pair is given a copy of the 'collated mistakes' worksheet. The teacher invites students to look through the document and see if they can identify why these mistakes are mistakes and what needs to be done in each case to both rectify the individual mistake and to avoid this type of mistake in the future.

After sufficient time has passed, the teacher leads a whole-class discussion in which different pairs share their thoughts. The teacher then hands out a second worksheet. This is the same as the first except it also includes annotations made by the teacher explaining why each mistake is a mistake, how to rectify these and how to avoid mistakes of that type in the future.

The teacher now leads a discussion in which students compare their thoughts with the teacher's expert feedback.

This method helps students to think carefully about mistakes and gives them detailed access to your expert thinking – a type of feedback which is particularly useful for them.

Pre-Hand-In Checklists

34 We touched on the idea of careless mistakes earlier (Entry 31). We noted that one of the benefits of teaching students about these is that they are then better placed to spot them in their own work. It is about giving students agency. We want them to do more effective self-assessment and to play a greater role in the quality control of what they produce.

Pre-hand-in checklists are another technique through which you can achieve similar ends. Create a checklist you would like all students to work through before they hand their work in. Emphasise that the purpose of the checklist is for students to increase the quality of their work prior to you looking at it. This allows you to concentrate on deeper and more meaningful aspects of the work, rather than on correcting a series of careless mistakes.

Here is an example of a checklist from primary school literacy:

Before you hand your work in:

- Check you have used capital letters.

- Check you have used full stops.

- Are there any sentences which don't make sense?

Repeated use of such a checklist habituates students into checking these points automatically. The teacher is saved a great deal of time when marking student work and can give feedback which is qualitatively different from what they might otherwise provide.

Checklist Training

35 As noted in the last entry, effective use of checklists depends in part on students being trained to use them. Here are some strategies you can use to do just that:

- **You check mine and I'll check yours.** Challenge students to check each other's work before it gets handed in. This helps students become familiar with the checklist. It also gives them access to what a peer notices about their work.

- **Double check.** Provide enough time so that students can check their work through twice. Indicate you want to see evidence of the second check. One way to do this is to add an additional criterion to the list for use during the second phase.

- **Reverse check.** Ask students to use the checklist in reverse order. This means they have to think actively about the checklist; it is a good way to avoid passive application (a common problem once students are familiar with a list).

- **Show me you've checked.** Indicate that students must find a way of demonstrating they have checked their work. This could see them using a different coloured pen to make changes or writing a brief summary explaining what they've identified through their checking.

- **Check Plus One.** Ask students to apply the checklist and to then add one extra criterion of their own. They should make a note of what this is so that, when you mark their work, you know what they also decided to look for.

Three Before Me

36 Three before me commonly refers to a strategy designed to encourage independent learning. Students are asked to consult three sources in an effort to answer their question before taking that question to the teacher. Often, the three sources are a book, a peer and themselves. It is a nice technique through which to promote agency and to reduce the likelihood that students automatically ask for help without first trying to work things out for themselves.

We can take the principle of the technique and apply it to marking to achieve similar ends. For some pieces of work, why not ask students to do 'three before me' prior to handing it in or asking for feedback? Here's an example of what it looks like in practice:

In a PE lesson, students are developing gymnastics routines. The teacher is circulating while learners work in groups. They make clear that they are on hand to give feedback, but that feedback will only be forthcoming if students have first self-assessed their routines, then taken feedback from a peer, and, finally, used one of the class IPads to compare their routine to that of a professional gymnast.

Clearly such an approach takes a bit of preparation and perhaps some training as well. However, in the above example we see students taking greater control over their work and can imagine that when the teacher does give feedback it is on a routine which has already been improved and developed.

Anonymous Marking

37 This is an unusual idea, one which sometimes yields little insight but, at other times, gives rise to surprising findings.

Set students a piece of work you intend to take in and assess. Create a set of paper slips, enough for one per student, each containing a different number. Hand out the slips at random. Ask students to write their number on their work, but not their name. They should also make a note of their number somewhere safe (for example, in a planner).

Take student work in and mark it as you normally would. Give feedback in the normal way and then, in a subsequent lesson, return student work by calling out numbers and asking students to claim what is theirs.

The purpose of using this technique is to see whether any unconscious biases are influencing your marking. For example, you might have unwittingly fallen into a routine of giving certain types of feedback to certain students. Of course, this might prove not to be the case, but using this method is a good way to check.

One limitation is that you might recognise student handwriting. This is hard to avoid. If you have access to computers you can ask students to type their work, thereby eliminating this factor.

It can be really interesting to find out whether you are bringing preconceptions to your marking. It can also be interesting for students to see whether this method results in different kinds of feedback from what they are used to receiving.

Annotated Exemplar Work

38 Exemplar work can be a form of feedback because it gives students access to what success looks like. The feedback is undirected and isn't personalised. Students need to compare the exemplar work with their own and make decisions about how to use the information it reveals. For this reason it is a loose form of feedback rather than a strong one.

You can increase the efficacy of exemplar work by annotating it with examples of how students can use the insights revealed. This gives student interaction with the exemplar work greater direction. Your annotations are a stronger form of feedback than the exemplar work offers in isolation. Students still have to decide what they will take from it, but this decision is made easier by your annotations.

For example, a history teacher might share an exemplar essay with students, along with annotations such as the following:

- Could you take this approach and use it in your own essay writing?

- Have you thought about starting your essays in this way? What difference might it make?

- How might you use source analysis like this to strengthen your arguments?

- Is this type of example one you could have included in your last essay? What difference would it have made?

- What difference would doing this make to your essay writing?

Having led the class in a discussion of the essay, they would then ask students to choose one annotation and use this to improve their next piece of work.

Annotated Mistakes

39 As with annotated exemplar work, so too with annotated mistakes. It is again about giving students access to our expertise so they can take that information and make it a part of their own understanding. Here are two examples of annotated mistakes being used to give students feedback:

- In a drama lesson, the teacher plays a video of themselves reciting a monologue. As students watch the teacher draws attention to a series of deliberate mistakes they made as part of their recitation. Students are then given a hand out containing a brief summary of the 'annotated' mistakes. They use this to help inform their own efforts. Here the feedback has come before the event.

- In a science lesson, the teacher gives students a handout containing data from an experiment along with three incorrect conclusions made about the data. Each conclusion is annotated with an explanation of why it is incorrect. This is supplemented by references to the data. The teacher talks students through the mistakes and then invites them to write up an experiment they conducted in a previous lesson, while trying to avoid making the same mistakes. Again, the feedback comes in advance of the event.

Annotated Grade Exemplifiers

40 How can we give students feedback about what constitutes work of a certain grade? One way is to provide annotated grade exemplifiers. That is, model pieces of work demonstrating what is required to reach a certain grade, supplemented by annotations explaining why different elements of the work are rewarded, gain marks or match the demands of the mark-scheme.

For example, a media studies lesson might see the teacher sharing three pieces of work with students:

- An annotated exemplar of a C grade piece of work.

- An annotated exemplar of a B grade piece of work.

- An annotated exemplar of an A grade piece of work.

They would invite students to discuss the exemplars in pairs before talking the whole class through some of their annotations and the key differences between the three pieces. The aim is to give students feedback in advance on what they need to do to take their work from a D to a C, a C to a B and a B to an A.

There is much similarity with Entry 38 – annotated exemplar work. They key difference is that here we are interested in helping students to understand what is necessary to achieve certain grade boundaries. As such, it is often of most use around exam time when students are seeking to make tweaks and enhancements to their work to meet the demands of the upcoming exams.

Target Implementation Time

41 Ensuring students have time in which they can implement their targets is vital. Without this, your feedback will probably have far less of an impact. Think about it from your own perspective. If a colleague observes you, gives you feedback and you then have no time in which to implement this, what happens? The feedback fades into the ether. The information is lost but, more importantly, the chance to improve has gone as well.

There are various ways in which you can ensure target implementation time. We'll look at some specific examples in the next seven entries. Before we do, here are a few questions to consider:

- Do you include target implementation time in your schemes of work?

- How much time do you put aside for students to think about, discuss and interpret your feedback?

- Do you ever have time to model and scaffold the feedback you give to students?

- How much of a priority is target implementation time? Does getting through the content always rank higher? If so, is this necessarily the right option?

- When was the last time you and your students focussed exclusively on discussing and acting on the feedback you provide (written or verbal)?

These are questions you can ask yourself periodically to prompt reflection on how feedback is being used in your lessons; and whether or not students are being given opportunities to make effective use of it.

Write – Do – Reflect

42 This is our first target implementation technique:

Students write their target at the top of their piece of work. They then attempt to put their target into practice as they do their work. Finally, they write a reflective paragraph explaining the extent to which they have successfully implemented their target. This may also include reflection on why this was difficult, where they failed and what they might try next time.

You can adapt it for non-writing activities:

At the start of a dance activity, students remind themselves of their most recent target, tell a partner what this is and say how they intend to implement it. They then take part in the activity, while working on their target, before reflecting on how successful they were in discussion with their partner.

In each case, we see targets placed front and centre. Student attention is focussed on them, avoiding the risk that the task takes over, pushing the target into the background. The reflective element at the end helps to promote a metacognitive engagement with the work. It also gives students a chance to identify what they might do next time if, on this occasion, implementation has proved difficult.

D.I.R.T.

43 This stands for Directed Improvement and Reflection Time. If you Google 'dirt teaching' you will find lots of resources and examples teachers and schools have shared via the internet.

The premise is simple. You specify a section of your lesson in which no new content is taught. Instead, everybody's sole focus is on improvement and reflection. The time has a red box around it, meaning that it never gets superseded by anything else. It is a way of ensuring that you build guaranteed target implementation time into your lessons.

For example, an English teacher might decide that every fourth lesson will begin with twenty minutes of D.I.R.T. In this time, students are expected to practice implementing their targets. For example, by rewriting elements of their work. At the same time, the teacher circulates through the room, scaffolding and modelling for students who are struggling to make sense of the most recent feedback they've been given.

Another option is to use D.I.R.T. as an opportunity for students to reflect on how their work has improved and whether or not they are in need of a new target. This is another way to help students take greater ownership of their learning. You are giving them the chance to decide when more feedback is required; something which is usually only in the hands of the teacher.

Activity – Feedback – Activity

44 Our third target implementation technique works as follows:

Set up an activity for the whole class to complete. As the activity unfolds, circulate and observe what students are doing. Listen in to conversations and analyse any work that is being produced. Before the activity finishes, use the information you collect to identify three key pieces of feedback relevant to the whole class.

Conclude the activity, deliver these pieces of feedback, along with an explanation of why they matter, and then lead students in a brief discussion (to help them make sense of and begin applying the ideas). Then, introduce a second activity, with similarities to the first, and ask students to complete this while implementing some or all of the feedback you have just shared.

Structuring a section of your lesson in this way means creating an opportunity to give feedback and an opportunity for students to instantly act on that feedback. Doing this repeatedly helps students to make quick gains. In essence, you are facilitating directed practice, with that direction informed by the feedback you provide.

It is worth noting that it is sometimes not possible to deliver three pieces of feedback which apply to the whole class. In these case, it is better to give separate feedback to individual students rather than bombard the whole class with an extended list of five or six pieces of information.

Target Trackers

45 A target tracker is a sheet of paper on which students record the targets or feedback you give them. They keep this sheet somewhere easily accessible and can then refer to it during lessons, at the start of activities, prior to beginning a piece of work and so on. They can also use the sheet to track their progress over time. This can help students to see whether they are successfully improving the quality of their work or whether they are getting stuck on the same things again and again.

Without a target tracker sheet there is the possibility that written feedback will get lost within student books or will disappear as pieces of paper are filed away in folders. A tracker sheet collates feedback, storing it in a single place which the student can access with ease. For example, a tracker sheet could be stuck onto the inside cover of a book, or kept at the very front of a folder.

Some teachers choose to write feedback directly into a target tracker sheet. Others write the feedback next to student work and then ask students to transfer this to the tracker sheet. Arguably, this second method ensures students have to think actively about the feedback they have been given, although there is always the possibility that they will copy it unthinkingly.

Finally, you might like to include a column on the sheet which students can fill in when they have successfully implemented a target. An extension is to have two columns – one to signal success from the student's perspective and one which the teacher signs off when, and only when, they agree with the student's self-assessment.

Practice Testing

46 Practice testing involves recreating exam-style conditions, but with low or no stakes attached. Examples include: flashcard testing, completing practice questions in class, low stakes mock exams and so forth.

Research (Dunlosky et al 2013) has suggested practice testing is one of the most effective ways to embed learning and improve recall. This tallies with the experience of many teachers and students, who know from experience that practising what will happen in exam conditions is an almost certain way to improve performance.

You can take practice testing a step further by combining it with target implementation. For example, you might observe a pair of students testing each other using flashcards. On listening to them, you notice they are getting most things right, but that they could give more detail when explaining the meaning of keywords. So, you give them this feedback and ask them put it into practice straightaway.

This neatly exemplifies how target implementation can be woven into practice testing, enhancing its efficacy and letting students focus their efforts on mastering the feedback you've provided.

Another example might see the teacher setting students a series of five practice questions, each one similar in structure but different in content. After each question, they provide feedback – perhaps to the class as a whole – which students try to implement on their next attempt.

Spaced Practice

47 In Dunlosky et al's study (see previous entry) spaced practice (sometimes known as distributed practice) also scored highly in terms of the positive impact it has on recall and the embedding of information in long-term memory. Spaced practice is similar to practice testing except here there is a gap between each successive period of practice. In short, practice is broken up into a series of short sessions over an extended period of time.

So, for example, a primary school teacher might decide that his class will do twenty minutes of handwriting practice at the start of every day, for a period of two weeks. He then decides to give students feedback at the start of every third session. Learners then have a chance to implement this feedback, using it to tailor their effort so that this is more in line with what is required. Again, we see an example of how to build target implementation time into lessons.

Another example could be a maths teacher who decides to use the first ten minutes of each lesson for mental arithmetic practice. Over the course of a term, they give students a series of targets to focus on, one at a time. At the start of each practice period, they remind students of the current target.

Again, we have a situation in which students are actively targeting their efforts in pursuit of feedback implementation.

Semantic Interrogation

48 Semantic interrogation is another technique that scored well in Dunlosky et al's research (though not as well as practice testing or spaced practice). This sees students interrogating information in order to attach meaning to it. The student looks at what is in front of them and asks 'why?' In searching for an answer they engage actively with the material. On finding an answer they can attach this to the information and enhance the possibility of recall.

We can apply the same principle when giving students targets. We can ask them to consider why they have been given a particular target – to interrogate their target in search of meaning. They may need some support here; and some students may need you to provide quite a lot of scaffolding. But when they have their meaning they will also have a reason explaining why they have received this particular target.

Three things follow. First, the activity sees students analysing and evaluating their target. This helps them to better understand it. Second, they now have a reason to pursue the target, which is often motivational. Three, they are more likely to remember their target because they have been through the process of attaching meaning to it.

Verbal Articulation of Target Self-Assessment

49 Here is a useful process you can teach students to help them self-assess whether or not they have successfully achieved a target. It works as follows:

Display a slide on the board containing some or all of the following questions:

- How have you tried to achieve your target?

- What has worked? Why did it work? What evidence do you have that it worked?

- What did you try that didn't work? Why didn't it work? What changes could you make?

- What was easy and what was difficult?

- How would you convince me that you are ready for a new target?

- What do you need to do next to achieve your target?

Give students 1-2 minutes of silent thinking time in which to reflect on these questions. Indicate that students are free to make notes if they want. When the time is up, ask students to get into pairs and to label themselves A and B. Indicate that, to begin with, A should interview B. They ask each question in turn and listen to their partner's answer. Students then swap roles. Finally, a bit of time is provided in which students can come out of role and discuss freely.

This process sees you leading students in a guided reflection. One which includes an opportunity to verbally articulate the results of that reflection. This process helps to embed student understanding at the same time as it allows students to refine and edit their thinking.

Internalisation of Criteria

50 We conclude our journey through feedback and marking with an overarching thought about what is happening when you consistently share your expertise with students and give them time in which to act on this.

One way to think about this is that students are slowly internalising the set of criteria you use to make expert judgements about their work, at that point in their school careers. The aim is to help students get closer and closer to an understanding of good which matches (or possibly even surpasses) your own understanding.

So, for example, we can imagine that a Year 8 geography teacher, through feedback and marking, is helping their students to develop an understanding of what good looks like in their subject, at this level of the curriculum, which is more and more in line with their own, expert, understanding. They are helping students to internalise the criteria of judgement; and will no doubt achieve this to greater and lesser extents across the board.

You may agree with this conceptualisation or not. But I personally find it a useful way in which to think about the processes of marking, of giving feedback, and of ensuring that feedback is understood and implemented. It indicates a gradual transfer of expertise from one mind (the teacher's) to another (the student's). Which, I would say, is a nice way to sum up learning in general.

And with that we draw our journey to a close. All that remains for me to say is that I hope you have enjoyed the book, that you have found the ideas useful, and that you can see ways in which you can take them and adapt them to suit your teaching style and the particular group of learners with whom you work. Finally, let me wish you all the best for developing your feedback and marking in the future. I'm sure you'll do a great job.

A Brief Request

If you have found this book useful I would be delighted if you could leave a review on Amazon to let others know.

If you have any thoughts or comments, or if you have an idea for a new book in the series you would like me to write, please don't hesitate to get in touch at mike@mikegershon.com.

Finally, don't forget that you can download all my teaching and learning resources for **FREE** at www.mikegershon.com and www.gershongrowthmindsets.com

47917841R00065

Printed in Poland
by Amazon Fulfillment
Poland Sp. z o.o., Wrocław